Who Was David Bowie?

by Margaret Gurevich

illustrated by Andrew Thomson

Penguin Workshop

To Stu and Noah, who love me as I am—MG

For Rhia and Cerys—AT

PENGUIN WORKSHOP
An imprint of Penguin Random House LLC, New York

First published in the United States of America by Penguin Workshop,
an imprint of Penguin Random House LLC, New York, 2021

Visit us online at penguinrandomhouse.com.

Library of Congress Cataloging-in-Publication Data is available.

Printed in the United States of America

ISBN 9781524787561 (paperback)   10 9 8 7 6 5 4 3 2 1 WOR
ISBN 9781524787578 (library binding)   10 9 8 7 6 5 4 3 2 1 WOR

Contents

Who Was David Bowie?

When audiences tuned in to their favorite British music show, *Top of the Pops*, on July 6, 1972, they didn't know what to expect from the singer they were about to see. Most had heard "Space Oddity," his huge hit that had actually been broadcast in Britain during the US Apollo 11 moon landing three years before. Some viewers had also bought his two most recent albums, *Hunky Dory* and *The Rise and Fall of Ziggy Stardust and the Spiders from Mars*. However, many people had never seen David Bowie perform live. They didn't even know what he looked like.

Then David stepped up to the mic. His hair was bright red, and he wore a rainbow-colored shiny jumpsuit and red boots. He also wore makeup. The audience wasn't sure what to think, but he certainly had their attention.

He grabbed the mic to sing "Starman," a song from the *Ziggy* album. As he sang, he put his arm around his guitarist, Mick Ronson. Some people were uncomfortable. They weren't used to seeing men wearing makeup on television. They also didn't like that David was hugging another man.

But he didn't care what they thought. He was only being himself. He pointed at the television audience as he sang. Viewers felt like he was talking to them and, just maybe, giving them permission to be themselves, too. It really felt as if he were speaking personally to everyone who was watching.

That night, the man in the blue eye shadow and sparkly clothes, dressed as Ziggy, a character from his most recent album, strummed his blue guitar and showed Britain who he was.

It had taken him nine years to become this successful. It was finally happening—and on his own terms.

CHAPTER 1
Absolute Beginners

David Robert Jones was born in Brixton, in South London, England, on January 8, 1947. He  had two older siblings, a half sister, Annette, and a half brother, Terry. His parents were Haywood Stenton Jones, called "John," and Margaret Mary Burns, known as "Peggy." John worked for a children's charity called Barnardo's, and Peggy worked as a waitress. When David was six, he and his parents moved to the Bromley neighborhood of London. Shortly after, Annette moved away, and Terry joined the air force.

At that time, parts of England were still recovering from World War II. Rubble littered the streets, and David and his friends sometimes played in old bomb shelters. David's childhood

was a happy one. His parents always encouraged music. Peggy spoke about David's grandfather, who played wind instruments. His father bought a record player—something few families could afford. In elementary school, David participated in art and music classes and sang in the choir.

He also loved all things American—even baseball and American football, which were both unpopular in England. His favorite music was American, too. He and his cousin Kristina often danced to records by Elvis Presley, a famous American singer.

Rock and Roll

Rock and roll became widely popular in the United States in the mid 1950s. With its roots in country music and rhythm and blues, it included musical instruments such as electric guitars, drums, electric bass, piano, saxophones, and trumpets.

Elvis Aaron Presley (1935–1977) was an American singer, musician, and actor who was called "the King of Rock and Roll." During one television appearance, he was only shown from the waist up because some people found his dancing inappropriate. Elvis recorded dozens of albums and hit songs, including "Heartbreak Hotel" and "Jailhouse Rock." He further popularized music that originated in Black communities and made rock and roll famous throughout the world.

Around this time, David's mother took him to see the American rock and roll artist Little Richard perform in a movie. That show sparked his interest in the saxophone. Shortly after, he begged his father to loan him money for the instrument. He worked part-time jobs to earn the rest. That Christmas, David finally received his saxophone. It was white with gold keys.

When David was eleven, Terry returned. He introduced David to jazz, a popular American music known for its improvised sound. When musicians improvise, they make up notes as they play, rather than playing something they've already memorized.

That year, David graduated from elementary school. For his secondary school, he chose Bromley Technical High School because of its music and art classes. He and his friends played their guitars at lunch and performed in an end-of-the-year school concert.

When he was sixteen, David saw his first live music performance—it was Little Richard.

He loved how Little Richard jumped on stage and stood on his white grand piano. At one point, he clutched his heart and fell to the floor. David thought Little Richard was dying. Suddenly, the performer raised his head and shouted, "Awopbopaloobop Alopbamboom!" The audience cheered. David never forgot that exciting performance.

In addition to the saxophone, David also learned to play the ukulele and piano. He and his friends sometimes made their own instruments and formed a band called the Konrads. One day, David and another band member, George Underwood, got into a fight. George punched

The Konrads

David right in the eye! After four months in the hospital and many surgeries, his left pupil looked much larger than his right. His eyes looked like they were two different colors. George felt awful, but David forgave him. His unique eyes became his favorite feature!

In 1963, all sixteen-year-old David wanted to do was sing and play instruments. He imagined himself wowing audiences just like Little Richard. That year, David graduated high school and began working in an advertising company. But the work—cutting and pasting designs on paper—was boring to him. He looked forward to evenings when he could play with the Konrads. Unfortunately, the late nights tired him out the next morning. David realized he couldn't be a rock star and work in an office, too. He quit the agency and formed a new band called Davie Jones and the King Bees.

David was the saxophone player and lead singer. He dreamed of making it big. His father also had huge hopes for him. He helped David write a letter asking companies to manage the King Bees. One of his letters compared the King Bees to the Beatles—the most popular

rock group in the world at that time. David's confidence worked! Leslie Conn, a talent scout, asked the King Bees to audition. Unfortunately, the band played so badly, he stopped them mid-set. David was so upset, he cried. But even if he

Davie Jones and the King Bees

Leslie Conn

didn't know what it was, Leslie saw *something* in the King Bees and decided to manage them, anyway.

In 1964, the King Bees put out a single called "Liza Jane." It flopped, and David searched for a new band again. He joined the Manish Boys in 1965. At the time, the "mod" look was in style. Mods dressed in three-piece suits, ties, and fancy shoes. David decided this should be the image of a lead singer.

But he needed more than style to get noticed. Leslie knew good stories got attention and helped David create his own. He appeared

vocalion
POP
45 R.P.M.

LIZA JANE
DAVIE JONES with THE KING BEES

on television and talked about how people made fun of his long hair. It wasn't true, but it got the Manish Boys extra publicity. Unfortunately, it wasn't enough to make them successful, and David once again searched for a new band.

He found a group called the Lower Third and a manager named Ken Pitt. Since there already was a well-known singer named Davy Jones in a band called the Monkees, Ken asked David to change his last name—but only for his career. His real name remained David Jones. He picked the name Bowie, after Jim Bowie, an American pioneer. He thought the name made him sound tough.

Jim Bowie even had a knife named after him! David called it "the ultimate American knife." With a new name and mod style, David hoped his career would reach new heights, too.

The Lower Third

CHAPTER 2
Who Can I Be Now?

David was twenty years old, and things were looking up. In 1967, Deram Records, a new music company, gave him a solo recording contract. This meant they only wanted David, not his band, the Lower Third. But David could finally create the music he liked best. Around the same time, David's half brother, Terry, began suffering from mental-health issues and had to move to a hospital for treatment. David missed Terry very

much. He tried to cope with Terry's absence by writing music.

The result was a new album called simply *David Bowie*. Like his other records, it did poorly. Ken Pitt didn't want him to give up, so he encouraged David to audition for theater and television. He landed parts in a short film and an ice cream commercial, but they paid little. His dreams of becoming a star were slipping away, and he explored other interests.

He studied with a famous mime, Lindsay Kemp, and started a musical group called Feathers.

Lindsay Kemp

In Feathers, David sang and performed as a mime. Ken saw this as another promotional opportunity. He created *Love You till Tuesday*, a thirty-minute film project showcasing David and his group. But it didn't bring stardom. Deram Records dropped him from their label. However, there was one person who *was* drawn to his Feathers performance—a woman named Mary Angela Barnett, who was called "Angie."

Angie was immediately charmed by David's singing voice and saw his star potential. The two soon began dating. David's personal life was changing, and he wanted a musical change, too. In 1969, he cofounded the Arts Lab, a safe space for musicians, poets, and singers to share their work without judgment. David shared his own music with others at the Arts Lab.

David and Angie Barnett

He'd just seen a movie called *2001: A Space Odyssey* about a journey to the moon and Jupiter. The storyline and special effects inspired him to write a song he called "Space Oddity." It was about an astronaut named Major Tom who was lost in space ". . . far above the world." Ken pitched this song to Mercury Records, a new label. They signed David to record a single and three albums.

2001: A Space Odyssey

2001: A Space Odyssey was released in movie theaters in 1968. The movie, produced and directed by Stanley Kubrick, was about a space voyage and aliens. But it also looked at how technology affected people and how that might unfold in the future. Critics praised its special effects.

It made more money than any other movie in North America in 1968, and Stanley Kubrick won an Academy Award for visual effects. In 2010, it was named the greatest film of all time by *The Moving Arts Film Journal*, an online magazine.

David's song "Space Oddity" was off to a slow start. That same year, the United States was planning its own space mission, Apollo 11. *Columbia* was the first spacecraft to take humans to the moon. Even though the song was released on July 11, 1969, British and American radio stations didn't want to play it until the astronauts returned safely to Earth. But Ken's friends at a British station did him a favor. When the astronauts placed the United States flag on the moon on July 20, 1969,

"Space Oddity" played on British televisions everywhere. It didn't hit the airwaves again until the astronauts returned to Earth four days later.

Just days after "Space Oddity" played on televisions, David competed in the Malta International Song Festival in Malta, Greece. Unfortunately, his second-place finish was followed by terrible news: His father was very sick. David flew home and showed him the award. John Jones had always supported his son and said he knew he'd succeed. He died shortly after, on August 5.

David was heartbroken. He said, "There were so many things I would have loved to have said." To escape the grief, he worked harder than ever.

While "Space Oddity" only hit 124 on the US music charts, by September it reached 48 in the

United Kingdom. David and Angie celebrated by moving out of David's parents' house and renting an apartment in Haddon Hall, a historic mansion in the English countryside. They hoped to make the place more stylish. They painted the sitting room and bedroom ceilings silver, the living-room walls a dark green, and the bedroom

Haddon Hall

walls pink. They covered the chairs in red velvet and dyed the drapes the same color. Finally, they built a recording studio in the basement.

Angie encouraged David's career, and he liked that she understood him so well. The couple married on March 19, 1970.

Angie made David happy, but his business partnership with Ken didn't. "Space Oddity" had reached number five in the United Kingdom a few months before, but David wanted to be well-known in the United States, too. He didn't think Ken was doing enough to make that happen. When Tony Defries promised stardom, David hired him as his new manager. He also started another band. Tony Visconti played bass and Mick "Woody" Woodmansey played drums. Mick "Ronno" Ronson became the guitarist. He had the popular hard-rock sound David wanted. The two became good friends, and Mick Ronson moved into Haddon Hall with him and Angie. With a new manager and band, David was ready for another new look.

Mick Ronson

The band wore silver jumpsuits, and David wore a silver-blue cape and dyed his hair to match. He and his bandmates also put on glittery makeup. The audience wasn't sure if it liked the dramatic new look, an extreme version of what was then called "glam rock," but the band was having fun.

David and his bandmates recorded their next album in April 1970. *The Man Who Sold the World* was one of the first glam-rock records to hit the music scene.

David was excited to shoot the cover photo for the album. He wore a blue-and-gold man's dress in a medieval style and lay on a lounge chair in his living room. He said the look was "very much" him. But American executives at Mercury Records didn't want a man wearing a dress on their album cover. David became angry, but it  didn't change things. In the end, the US cover had a picture of a cowboy, and the UK cover had the photo of David at home in Haddon Hall.

Glam Rock

Glam rock, also called glitter rock, became popular in the early 1970s. Unlike performers before them who wore suits or T-shirts and jeans, glam bands liked sparkly, flashy clothes. Musicians wore colorful makeup and wigs, and they dyed their hair bright shades. They also wore high-heeled shoes and jumpsuits in metallic colors.

Other famous glam bands were New York Dolls, Roxy Music, and T. Rex.

Marc Bolan of T. Rex

CHAPTER 3
The Man Who Sold the World

Even though *The Man Who Sold the World* didn't quite get David the fame he was hoping for in Britain, Mercury Records set up a multistate radio tour in the United States. David was interviewed by radio hosts and sang his songs for listeners. The performances weren't live concerts, but he was excited to finally travel to the country of his dreams.

His whirlwind twelve-city tour began in Washington, DC, on January 25, 1971. With such a tight schedule, David didn't have much time to sightsee. However, he did get to see the Velvet Underground perform in New York City on January 27. David loved the band's sound and their lyrics, and he was especially impressed with the bandleader, Lou Reed. Lou sang, wrote songs, and played guitar—just like David.

Lou Reed

When his US radio tour ended on February 14, David returned to London. Angie was pregnant and couldn't travel with him, so he was glad to be home. He was also excited to work on his fourth album, called *Hunky Dory*.

The Velvet Underground

The Velvet Underground was an American rock band formed in 1965. The band included John Cale, Sterling Morrison, Angus MacLise, and later Moe Tucker and Nico. It was led by its singer, songwriter, and guitarist, Lou Reed. It was very different from more "happy" rock groups of the time. Andy Warhol, a Pop artist who was known for his unique paintings—like images of tomato soup cans—managed the band.

In 1996, the Velvet Underground was inducted into the Rock and Roll Hall of Fame. In 2004, *Rolling Stone* magazine ranked the band number nineteen among the one hundred greatest artists of all time.

One month after David began recording *Hunky Dory*, Angie gave birth to their son. Duncan Zowie Haywood Jones was born on May 30, 1971, at Bromley Hospital. Angie and David called him Zowie, which means "life" in Greek. With another album almost complete and a new role as a dad, David was ready for whatever came next.

CHAPTER 4
Ziggy Stardust

In August 1971, David completed *Hunky Dory* and flew to New York City to sign with RCA, a record company that represented famous singers like Elvis Presley. It rolled out the star treatment David had always wanted and filled his hotel room with Elvis Presley records. It also hosted a dinner in David's honor—and Lou Reed joined them. That night, David also met famous singer and songwriter Iggy Pop. Lou, Iggy, and David became good friends.

Iggy Pop (1947–)

James Newell Osterberg Jr., known as Iggy Pop, is an American singer, songwriter, musician, and actor. He was born in Muskegon, Michigan. Iggy began playing drums in his teens and created the punk band the Psychedelic Stooges in 1967. The band was also known as Iggy and the Stooges, and simply the Stooges. Known for his energetic performances, Iggy was one of the first artists to stage dive into the audience. The Stooges became famous for their raw energy and hard-driving rock and roll, which led to Iggy becoming known as the "Godfather of Punk."

In 2010, he and the Stooges were inducted into the Rock and Roll Hall of Fame.

In September, David began work on his next album, *The Rise and Fall of Ziggy Stardust and the Spiders from Mars.* The album told the story of Ziggy Stardust, an alien rock star who was sent to Earth. David dressed up as Ziggy, and his bandmates dressed up as the Spiders from Mars. The band wore high-heeled boots; shiny gold, pink, and blue jumpsuits; and colored their hair to match. David's jumpsuit was red, blue, and gold. To complete the look, he wore red plastic boots, grew his hair long, and dyed it fire-engine red. He also wore makeup and painted his nails white.

David couldn't wait to show off his unique look, so he dressed as Ziggy for an interview with *Melody Maker* magazine. Even though he was married, David told the interviewer, "I'm gay and always have been . . ." This was a very bold thing to say in 1972. In Britain, being gay was considered a crime only six years earlier.

He was the first really famous person to say something like this about his personal life. But why did David say it? He didn't like to be labeled—and he didn't think other people should be, either. If he wanted to say he was gay, he did. If he wanted to be straight, he was. He wanted to be free to make that choice. And he just wanted to be himself.

The Rise and Fall of Ziggy Stardust and the Spiders from Mars was released in June 1972. One month later, the band performed on *Top of the Pops*, a popular British television show.

Wearing his Ziggy outfit and makeup, David gave a powerful live performance. He was as "far out" as his music.

David returned to the United States again and performed live in twenty-one cities. His songs played on US radio stations, and his shows were sold out!

In November 1972, *Rolling Stone*, a popular magazine that reports on the most influential musicians, politicians, and pop culture, put David on the cover. He was finally getting the recognition he felt he deserved.

David's sixth album, *Aladdin Sane*, was released shortly after, in April 1973. The cover showed David with a red-and-blue lightning bolt drawn down the center of his face.

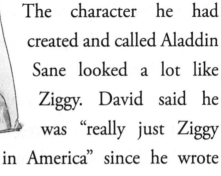

The character he had created and called Aladdin Sane looked a lot like Ziggy. David said he was "really just Ziggy in America" since he wrote all the songs on his US Ziggy Stardust Tour.

Aladdin may have looked a bit like Ziggy, but the album's sound was louder and livelier than David's others. Mike Garson, a new musician who had joined the band, had added bigger keyboard sounds and a jazzy piano solo. The band added more drums to their sound as well. Audiences loved it.

The album sold one hundred thousand advanced copies—a feat last accomplished by the Beatles—and entered the UK charts at number one! It was David's first number-one album, and it stayed there for five weeks. His earlier songs were rereleased and also became popular. Tony Defries arranged a promotional tour in Japan so new audiences could hear David's music.

David was very interested in Japanese culture and landmarks. He, Angie, and Zowie attended a sumo wrestling show, visited Japanese temples, and dined with Kabuki actors. One famous Kabuki actor, Bandō Tamasaburō V, helped David apply his makeup in a Japanese style. But David wasn't new to Japanese fashion. During some of his New York performances on the Ziggy Stardust Tour, he wore clothes created by Kansai Yamamoto, a famous fashion designer who had been inspired by Kabuki.

David with Kansai Yamamoto

Kabuki Theater

Kabuki theater began in Japan in 1603. A traditional form of Japanese dance and musical theater, it's known for its bright, detailed costumes, makeup, and music. The word *kabuki* comes from the Japanese words meaning "song," "dance," and "skill."

Although Kabuki began with female actors, now only male actors perform both the female and male roles. In 2006, the United Nations Educational, Scientific, and Cultural Organization (UNESCO) recognized Kabuki as an important part of Japan's cultural history.

Even though David enjoyed fame, he was tired of daily performances and traveling. Re-creating his Ziggy character night after night was exhausting. It took him five hours to put on his Ziggy makeup and one hour to remove it. A show in Earls Court, London, in May 1973,

was the last straw. Fans rushed the stage in the middle of his performance. Security had to stop the show for fifteen minutes. And this wasn't the first time the crowd had become rowdy. During many concerts, fans grabbed and ripped David's clothing. Performing became stressful.

On July 3 of that year, during a performance at Hammersmith Odeon in London, David made a surprise announcement in front of 3,500 fans.

He said, "This is the last show we'll ever do." The audience and his band were shocked. David just wanted to retire from Ziggy, but he wasn't sure what would come next. He needed time to figure it out.

CHAPTER 5
Diamond Dogs

Retired from performing with the Spiders from Mars, David's first step was to record a cover album. When musicians "cover" music, they sing other artists' songs, often by adding their own spin. David's cover album was called *Pin Ups*, and he chose songs from a wide variety of other bands and songwriters. Mick Ronson and Trevor Bolder, two former bandmates, played guitar and bass on the album. *Pin Ups* came out in October 1973 and reached number one in the United Kingdom.

Now David was even more popular. Fans camped out in front of his house. One even broke into Haddon Hall, and David and Angie had to call the police! They rented a new house on King's Road with no front courtyard for fans to gather in.

With fewer interruptions, David focused on his music again. On June 14, 1974, less than a year after his "last show," he and his band were ready to perform again. The tour of the United States and Canada showcased David's vocals, guitar skills, and yet another look. Instead of

glitter, bright colors, and vinyl boots, David wore dress pants, cotton shirts, suspenders, and sensible shoes. He also dyed his hair a natural red. Unlike his new style, the Diamond Dogs Tour design was his flashiest yet. David performed many songs suspended above the audience on a movable bridge. At one point, he emerged from an oversize hand! The set weighed six tons and cost over $400,000 to build. But David kept getting stuck in the air, and the bridge collapsed once with him on it! He stopped the tour in August to record the *Young Americans* album. When the tour restarted in October, the fancy props were gone, and it was renamed the Soul Tour. David played some songs from his unreleased album as well as his *Diamond Dogs* music.

David said the Diamond Dogs Tour was both "spectacular" and a "headache." Unfortunately, his personal life wasn't so spectacular. He was spending a lot of time away from Zowie and

Angie, and his marriage was suffering. He also found out that his manager, Tony Defries, was making a lot of money from his performances and albums, but David was earning little.

He decided to take another break from performing.

David's downtime worked in his favor. *Young Americans* debuted in March 1975. David had asked his old producer Tony Visconti to help produce the album. It included a song called

"Fame." Although it was missing David's usual instrumental sound, that September it became his first number-one hit in the United States. The song was also special because he cowrote it with his friend John Lennon and Puerto Rican musician Carlos Alomar.

Now that he had a number-one hit in the United States, David left his manager and decided to explore acting. He moved to Los Angeles, California, in April 1975, where he landed his first movie role. In *The Man Who Fell to Earth*,

he played Thomas Jerome Newton, an alien who comes to Earth to save his planet from a drought. Even though David received praise for his acting, the movie was not a success.

John Lennon (1940–1980)

John Lennon was a British singer, songwriter, and musician. His first band was called the Quarrymen. He went on to found the Beatles in 1960 with Paul McCartney, George Harrison, and Ringo Starr. The band broke up in 1970, but John continued to write music and record music. His most famous song, "Imagine," is about wanting peace in the world.

John was killed in December 1980 in New York City. People mourned for him all over the world. Strawberry Fields, an area of Central Park in New York City, is named after one of his songs and serves as a memorial for him today.

In addition to acting in the movie, David had originally agreed to record its soundtrack. But he was overworked and tired. After the movie finished production in August, he moved to Bel Air, a quiet area of Los Angeles. He hoped the change in scenery would help him focus on the soundtrack. Instead, he began recording songs for his new album, *Station to Station*. The songs had an electronic sound that was currently popular in German music. Electronic music uses synthesizers, computers, or tape recorders to change the sound of the music. The first song began with sounds of an oncoming train.

Station to Station was released in January 1976. It was his highest-charting album in the United States. To complement the album, David also created another character. The Thin White Duke was inspired by gentlemen from old, silent German movies. Because the movies were black and white, the Duke only wore those colors.

David dyed his hair blond and added a white shirt, white gloves, black vest, and black pants. Even the stage design matched. It was black except for a few white spotlights.

David toured from February through May, but he wasn't well. He and Angie weren't getting along. He was also not sleeping or eating very much. While in Los Angeles, he began experimenting with drugs in new and dangerous ways. As much as he loved creating new music, he knew he had to leave Los Angeles to get better. In August, David moved to Berlin, Germany, with Zowie.

David and son, Zowie, at home in Berlin, Germany

His personal secretary and best friend, Corinne "Coco" Schwab, came to help. His plan was to live life as a normal person and have "nothing to do with rock and roll."

CHAPTER 6
Brilliant Adventure

In Berlin, David read, painted, wrote music, and explored the city. He especially enjoyed art museums and galleries. He also spent a lot of time with five-year-old Zowie—something he didn't get to do when he was on tour. No one asked for his autograph, and he liked that he could roam Berlin without screaming fans. One night, he went to see a show and surprised the audience by getting on stage. Instead of cheering, they asked him to get down. They hadn't come to see *him*! David was glad no one thought he was special.

He also invited his good friend Iggy Pop to Berlin. He helped Iggy produce his albums *The Idiot* and *Lust for Life*, and he played the piano on Iggy's tour. David was more than happy to blend into the background. Most of the audience didn't even know it was him! He also became friends with another musician named Brian Eno.

David Bowie and Iggy Pop in Berlin

With the help of Eno and Tony Visconti, David began working on a series of albums known as the Berlin Trilogy. The first two albums, *Low* and *"Heroes,"* focused on moody, atmospheric music, rather than more standard types of rock and roll.

Brian Eno (1948–)

Brian Peter George Eno, often just called Eno, is an English musician and producer. He is known for experimenting with electronic sounds and creating ambient music, setting a mood by using different instrumental sounds. One of his most important albums is 1978's *Music for Airports*. He produced songs and albums for many bands, including U2, Talking Heads, Coldplay, Roxy Music, and David Bowie.

The third album, *Lodger*, returned to traditional guitar-based rock. Even though all three albums made the top forty on the billboard charts, none produced number-one hits.

That didn't matter to David. The city of Berlin had done what he had hoped it would do: helped him escape fame and become creative once again. David returned to London. He was excited to see where his life would take him. But by 1980, David and Angie had grown apart. They divorced in February.

In September of that year, David played the lead role in *The Elephant Man* on Broadway.

David's role, John Merrick, was based on a real person named Joseph Merrick who suffered from physical deformities. David studied everything he could about Merrick. He even visited the London hospital that  had Merrick's clothing. The hard work paid off. David's Broadway debut received high praise.

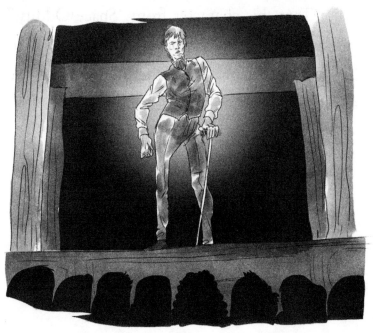

He followed his Broadway success with *Scary Monsters*, his fourteenth album. David used a technique called the "cut-up," which added sudden noise to songs. He said it was the "kind of music I really wish to make." He didn't worry about the album selling. But *Scary Monsters* did sell big—reaching number one in the United Kingdom.

One huge hit, "Ashes to Ashes," mentioned Major Tom, his character from "Space Oddity." Music videos weren't popular yet, but David directed a short movie for the song. It used the latest computer graphics.

"Ashes to Ashes" video

But a tragedy stopped David from touring with *Scary Monsters*. That December, his good friend John Lennon was murdered by a fan in New York City. He couldn't believe something so horrible could happen, and he worried about going out in public.

With no tour or record to work on, David found other ways to be creative. He loved working with various artists and became friends with Freddie Mercury, the lead singer of the British band Queen. Together they produced and cowrote the lyrics for "Under Pressure," a song that eventually reached number one in the United Kingdom.

In January 1983, David signed with EMI Records for around $17 million. He then released his newest album, *Let's Dance*. The single from the album, also called "Let's Dance," became David's first song to hit number one in both the United States and the United Kingdom. Even he was surprised! Two other songs on the

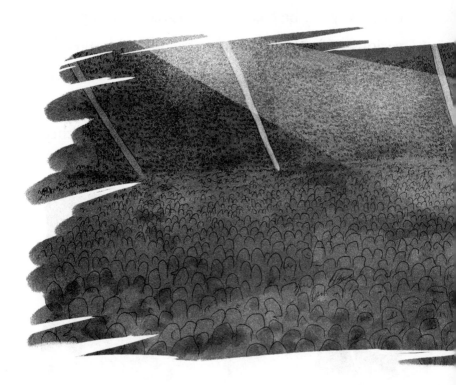

album, "Modern Love" and "China Girl," were big hits, too.

David was even more famous than before. His Serious Moonlight promotional tour covered sixteen countries and ninety-six shows! More than two and a half million fans attended.

Serious Moonlight Tour, 1983

But David wanted more than big hits. He wanted his songs to focus on important issues, like racism. He traveled to Australia to film videos for the songs "Let's Dance" and "China Girl." He said of both videos, "the message that they have is very simple—it's wrong to be racist!"

At thirty-six years old, David had more than he imagined. He was a devoted father to Zowie, and his musical career was doing better than ever. In July, ten of his albums had made it to the top hundred on the UK charts. The only artist to beat that record was Elvis Presley.

On January 16, 1985, David's half brother, Terry, died. David threw himself into his work to cope with the difficult loss.

In July, he was asked to participate in Live Aid—a concert to help the people in Ethiopia, a nation in Africa. Because of drought and civil war, many there were starving. People in the neighboring country of Sudan were starving, too. Bob Geldof, who was in an Irish band called the Boomtown Rats, organized the concert and invited many popular bands and singers to participate.

Bob Geldof

David was honored to be a part of Live Aid. He dedicated "Heroes," his biggest hit of the night, "to my son, to all our children, and to the children of the world." He also cut his set short to show a video of the famine in Ethiopia. As his band left the stage, he said, "Let us not forget why we are here. People are still starving." More money was pledged after the video aired than at any other time during the concert.

Onstage at Live Aid, 1985

CHAPTER 7
Changes

After Live Aid, David focused on producing, writing, and recording his best friend Iggy Pop's new album *Blah-Blah-Blah*. The album gave Iggy his first top-fifty US hit, "Real Wild Child (Wild One)," which was also a top-ten hit in the United Kingdom.

But David's own label, EMI, threatened to drop him if he didn't produce a new album soon. So, David forced himself to write. Some bandmates felt his heart wasn't into *Never Let Me Down*, his new record. Still, he had to go on tour to promote it. The result was the Glass Spider Tour—so called because David came out of a glass spider that hung above the stage!

Live Aid (July 13, 1985)

Live Aid was a sixteen-hour concert held at two locations: Wembley Stadium in London and JFK Stadium in Philadelphia. The concerts at both stadiums were broadcast by satellite to 110 nations around the world.

More than one billion viewers tuned in to see some of the world's most popular bands and singers, including Madonna, Elton John, U2, and Duran Duran. The band Queen's performance was one of the most memorable. Their twenty-one-minute set included their top hits, "Bohemian Rhapsody," "We Will Rock You," and "We Are the Champions." The whole stadium clapped for "Radio Ga Ga."

The concert raised more than $127 million. Bob Geldof was later knighted by Queen Elizabeth II.

On June 6, 1987, the tour took him again to Berlin. His concert was going to take place near the Berlin Wall, a barrier built to separate East and West Germany.

David's 1987 concert was on the West side of the wall, but people from the East were standing on their own side, listening and singing along,

too. "It was terribly emotional," David said. Many believed his song "Heroes" was about a man and woman whose lives were separated by the wall.

When the tour was over, he and his crew destroyed the glass spider. But he would always remember his life in Berlin ten years earlier and his concert at the Berlin Wall.

Berlin Wall (1961–1989)

When Germany was defeated at the end of
World War II, the entire country was split into four
sections. Each section was controlled by one of
the four winning powers: the United States, Great
Britain, France, and the Soviet Union. The United
States, Great Britain, and France controlled the part
of Germany that came to be known as West Germany.
The Soviet Union ruled over the section called East
Germany.

The relationship between the West and East
was unfriendly. People on the West side had many
more rights than people on the East. Many from the
East fled to the West. The Soviet Union wanted to
stop people from leaving East Germany. The city of
Berlin had been split into four sections, too. In 1961,
a wall was built separating West Berlin from East
Berlin. Guards patrolled the wall night and day, and

they seriously injured or killed anyone trying to cross.

The wall symbolized the different views: freedom on one side and harsh government restrictions on the other. The Berlin Wall was finally taken down in November 1989.

CHAPTER 8
Modern Love

David was a rock star, but he wasn't always happy. He felt a lot of pressure to write hit songs. One day, his friend Reeves Gabrels asked him if it mattered what people thought. He encouraged David to play the music that mattered to *him*. That conversation inspired David. He formed a new band in May 1989. It was called Tin Machine, and he was the lead singer. He asked Reeves to play guitar.

With David's creativity back on track, he longed

Reeves Gabrels

for someone with whom he could share his life and his success. In 1990, at a dinner party, he met famed fashion model Iman Abdulmajid. David liked her immediately, but Iman was nervous about dating a rock star. David showed her he didn't care about fame. Their first date was tea—easy and not fancy at all.

Iman Abdulmajid (1955–)

Iman Abdulmajid was born in Somalia and began her modeling career in 1976. She was one of the most successful models in the following decades. In 1992, she brought attention to Somalia's suffering. Her documentary, *Somalia Diary*, showed the effects of war and famine on the country.

In 1994, Iman teamed up with a makeup artist to create her own cosmetics line. Iman Cosmetics was one of the first skincare lines created for women of color. Iman's makeup line continued to grow with a brand called "I-Iman," which was made for women of all colors.

In addition to writing two books and creating a top-selling fashion accessory, jewelry, and handbag line for the Home Shopping Network, she also started a home decorating line called Iman Home. In 2010, the Council of Fashion Designers awarded her with the Fashion Icon Award.

They got married two years later on April 24, 1992, in Switzerland. It was a small ceremony for just the couple. Two months later, they had another wedding in Italy for their closest friends. Even though it rained, they couldn't be happier.

David's marriage to Iman inspired him. He was no longer with Tin Machine. His next album, *Black Tie White Noise*, was actually a tribute to his wedding. It began with the song "The Wedding" and ended with "The Wedding Song." The album came out in April and hit number one on the UK music charts.

David continued recording music, but touring exhausted him. Even without the visibility of those big tours, he was honored for his contributions to the music world. In 1996, he received a Brit Award for Lifetime Achievement and was inducted into the Rock and Roll Hall of Fame. David turned fifty on January 8, 1997. One day later, he marked the big day with a special event. He invited famous bands and singers including members of the Foo Fighters, Sonic Youth, and even Lou Reed— his musical hero—to sing with him on stage at Madison Square Garden. All proceeds went to the charity Save the Children.

In 2000, David and Iman had been married eight years. On August 15, 2000, they had their first child together, a daughter named Alexandria Zahra Jones. They called her Lexi.

The three of them moved to New York. Unlike in London, no one stopped them on the streets for autographs or to take photos.

The family lived in downtown Manhattan. On September 11, 2001, two planes hit the World Trade Center in a terrorist attack. David was on the phone with Iman when it happened. Their apartment was blocks from the site. He told Iman and Lexi to go to a safe place. Phones stopped working soon after. He couldn't talk to them until later that night. It was a very scary time. On October 20, David and other musicians performed in a concert at Madison Square Garden to raise money for the families of victims affected by the attacks and to honor all the first responders who had risked their lives on September 11.

CHAPTER 9
Golden Years

In September 2003, David was set to begin a tour for his new album, *Reality*. It was going to be his biggest tour in five years. But parts of the tour had to be cancelled when David developed laryngitis. A few months later, he became sick with the flu. Then, in June, a fan threw a lollipop in his left eye—the same eye George punched years ago! David kept his sense of humor. "Lucky you hit the bad one," he said.

But just a week later, David had a heart attack and collapsed backstage after a show. He focused on getting better and recording music. Two years later, on September 8, 2005, he performed in a benefit concert to aid the victims of Hurricane Katrina, a hurricane that devastated the state of Louisiana. He wore high-water pants, a bandage on his wrist, and black makeup around his eye. His costume was supposed to symbolize how badly Louisiana was hurt.

Although he was happy to devote time to the victims of Hurricane Katrina, David didn't enjoy being in the spotlight anymore. After receiving a Grammy Lifetime Achievement Award in 2006, he said, "I'm taking a year off—no touring, no albums."

That year turned into seven. On January 8, 2013, his sixty-sixth birthday, David released a new single and video, "Where Are We Now?" Listeners could download it immediately on iTunes. This was followed by *The Next Day*—his twenty-fourth studio album and his first in ten years. While it was a surprise to his fans, David had actually been recording for years. It became his first number-one album in the United Kingdom since *Black Tie White Noise*, and it was nominated for Best Rock Album at the 2014 Grammy Awards.

A year later, he released a greatest-hits collection and and once again turned his attention to the

Hurricane Katrina

Hurricane Katrina hit the Gulf Coast of the United States on August 23, 2005. Over 1,800 people died, and one million Americans were left homeless. New Orleans, Louisiana, was affected the most. Causing more than $160 billion in damage, Hurricane Katrina was the costliest storm ever for the United States. Parts of New Orleans are still damaged today. Because the storm was so devastating, the name Katrina was retired, never to be used for storms again.

theater. Instead of acting in a show, he wrote the music and lyrics to an off-Broadway musical called *Lazarus*. The show was about the same character he had played years earlier in *The Man Who Fell to Earth*.

In 2015, David began work on his next album, *Blackstar*. Just like *The Next Day*, it was recorded in secret in New York City. His old friend and producer, Tony Visconti, produced the album, and David hired local jazz musicians to play. The song "Blackstar" incorporated a saxophone solo, drums, blues, jazz, and acid house, a musical style that uses an electronic synthesizer. Although two of the songs on *Blackstar*, "Blackstar" and "Lazarus," were released in 2015, the album itself was not released until January 8, 2016, his sixty-ninth birthday. Critics praised the album, and fans thought that David was back for good. But his fans were proven wrong.

"Lazarus" video, 2016

David died in his home from liver cancer just two days later, on January 10. The world was in shock. Even many close to him hadn't known he was sick. David had kept his illness a secret because he wanted privacy. He didn't even want a public memorial or funeral.

David's music and style-setting clothes and characters influenced generations of performers, including Lady Gaga and Boy George. He was always willing to learn about new music and reinvent himself. Tony Visconti said, "He was a trailblazer" and "broke his own rules." He didn't like labels. He didn't want to explain himself to others—from the purse he carried to the relationships he had.

The video for "Lazarus" shows David in a hospital bed. He sings about being in heaven.

Some people believe this might have been David's way of saying goodbye.

Timeline of David Bowie's Life

1947 — David Robert Jones is born on January 8 in Brixton, London

1967 — First album, *David Bowie*, is released

1969 — Single "Space Oddity" is released

1970 — Marries Mary Angela "Angie" Barnett

1971 — Duncan Zowie Haywood Jones is born

1972 — *The Rise and Fall of Ziggy Stardust and the Spiders from Mars* is released

— Appears on the cover of *Rolling Stone*

1973 — Releases *Aladdin Sane*

1975 — "Fame" becomes first US number-one hit

— "Space Oddity" becomes first UK number-one hit

1979 — Releases Berlin Trilogy: *Low*, *"Heroes," Lodger*

1980 — Divorces Angie Barnett

1983 — "Let's Dance" hits number one in the United States and the United Kingdom

1985 — Performs at Live Aid

1992 — Marries Iman Abdulmajid

2000 — Alexandria Zahra Jones is born

2016 — Releases final album, *Blackstar*

— Dies from cancer on January 10 in New York City

Timeline of the World

1947 — Jackie Robinson becomes the first African American player on a major league baseball team

1951 — Color television introduced in the United States

1962 — Spider-Man comic book character debuts in Marvel Comics' *Amazing Fantasy* #15

1969 — Neil Armstrong becomes first man to walk on the moon

1973 — First mobile telephone is invented by Motorola researcher and executive Martin Cooper

1981 — Heavyweight champion boxer Muhammad Ali competes in his last fight

1997 — The first Harry Potter book, *Harry Potter and the Philosopher's Stone*, is published in the United Kingdom

1998 — Denver Broncos become first AFC team in fourteen years to win the Super Bowl

2007 — Nancy Pelosi becomes first female speaker of the US House of Representatives

2015 — US Supreme Court declares same-sex marriage a constitutional right

2016 — Simone Biles sets US record for most gold medals in women's gymnastics in a single Olympic Games

Bibliography

*Books for young readers

Buckley, David. *Strange Fascination: Bowie: The Definitive Story*. London: Virgin Books Ltd, 2005.

Egan, Sean. *Bowie on Bowie: Interviews and Encounters with David Bowie*. Chicago: Chicago Review Press, 2015.

*Forget, Thomas. *Rock & Roll Hall of Famers: David Bowie*. New York: The Rosen Publishing Group, Inc., 2002.

Johnson, Emily. "Kabuki and the Art of . . . David Bowie?" **Inside Japan**. Last accessed November 22, 2020. https://www.insidejapantours.com/blog/2016/01/11/kabuki-and-the-art-of-david-bowie/.

Jones, Dylan. *David Bowie: A Life*. New York: Penguin Random House, 2017.

Leigh, Wendy. *Bowie: The Biography*. New York: Gallery Books, 2014.

Light, Alan. " 'Ziggy Stardust': How Bowie Created the Alter Ego That Changed Rock." *Rolling Stone*, June 16, 2016. https://www.rollingstone.com/music/music-news/ziggy-stardust-how-bowie-created-the-alter-ego-that-changed-rock-55254/.

"Mod Culture." *Discover John Smedley.* https://www.johnsmedley.com/discover/community/mod-culture/.

Newman, Jason. "Bowie in the Outback: Inside Making of Groundbreaking 'Let's Dance' Video." *Rolling Stone*, April 14, 2016. https://www.rollingstone.com/movies/movie-news/bowie-in-the-outback-inside-making-of-groundbreaking-lets-dance-video-182691/.

Rose, Caryn. "Bowie's Live Aid magic: An unforgettable show, from the spine-tingling 'Heroes' to his audacious 'Dancing in the Street' duet." **Salon**. January 12, 2016. https://www.salon.com/2016/01/12/bowies_live_aid_magic_an_unforgettable_show_from_the_spine_tingling_heroes_to_his_audacious_lets_dance_duet/.

Trynka, Paul. *David Bowie: Starman*. New York: Little, Brown and Company, 2011.

Williams, Cameron. "How MTV Changed the World with Its Industry of Cool." **SBS**. February 13, 2017. https://www.sbs.com.au/guide/article/2017/02/13/how-mtv-changed-world-its-industry-cool.

Wolk, Douglas. "How David Bowie's 'Scary Monsters' Turned Avant-Rock Into Chart-Topping Pop." *Rolling Stone*, September 12, 2016. https://www.rollingstone.com/music/music-features/how-david-bowies-scary-monsters-turned-avant-rock-into-chart-topping-pop-121686/.